NOTEBOOK

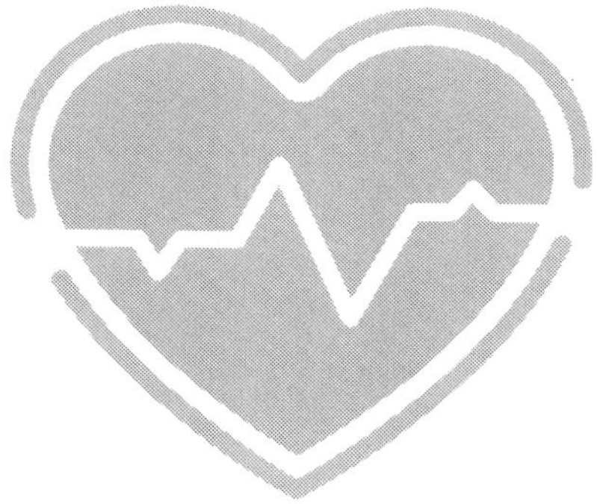

BELONGS TO:

PHONE:

E-MAIL: